AF464885

Better Than All The Rest

Doug McNaught

Contact bekasume.books@optusnet.com.au

ISBN: **978-1-84799-503-2**

Table of Contents

Introduction

I was reading one of those lifestyle magazines that come with a weekend newspaper recently and they were talking about meditation, of the transcendental kind. The article told how meditation was the key to improving a person's health and wellbeing. Its author added that Christians who pray for at least 30 minutes every day achieve the same sense of wellbeing.

In the final analysis, everyone wants to know real peace of mind, more than, say, fame and wealth. We, who love the Lord Jesus Christ, know that, "the peace of God, which transcends all understanding, will guard your hearts and your minds in Christ Jesus." (Philippians 4: 7 NIV)

When I was a student people used to say that religion was a crutch. People need a crutch when a limb is unsound. Jesus Christ, our Lord, is not a crutch, He is the sound limb, and everything else is a crutch.

Christians, like everyone else, want to know true inner peace, that is, the peace of God in their hearts. We were created to have a rich and fulfilling relationship with our Maker and in that relationship we can know true peace, the peace of God. In order to understand more about this peace, which is our right, freely given but at great cost, we need to know more about God. This book begins by looking into the God of the Old Testament and then introducing the Divine Saviour of the New Testament.

Each Christian should take time to enjoy the perfection of our Saviour; we could easily spend time competing with ourselves, in the privacy of our own minds, praising the Saviour more and more each day. From there it is but a short journey to knowing the peace of God in our hearts everyday of our lives. This book is designed to give each Christian some resources to praise our perfect Christ.

Ruth And Boaz

The book of Judges contains a sad refrain: "in those days there was no king in Israel." (Judges 17: 6; 18: 1; 19: 1; 21: 25) This indicates a time of lawlessness for this comment precedes the statement, "but every man did that which was right in his own eyes" twice and the other two times it tells a story of lawlessness.

Once before the story of the Tribe of Dan and how they tried to find their own land; (Judges 18) a disgraceful time when the men of Dan stole an idol and took the Levite who tended this idol to make him their own priest. These men then fell on the inhabitants of Laish, who were "quiet and secure: and they smote them with the edge of the sword, and burnt the city with fire."(Judges 18: 27 NIV) Dan did not take up its allotted inheritance but chose to go outside the place chosen by God and take their own inheritance and worship their own God. One wonders if this is the reason that Dan is the only tribe not mentioned among the one hundred and forty four thousand of Revelation 7.

On the second occasion, the men of Gibeah tried to rape a young man staying in their town, they were given his concubine and they raped the woman to death. After this the tribe of Benjamin fought against the rest of Israel and they were nearly annihilated. (See Judges 19, 20) These events illustrate the problems which occurred when there was no king in Israel This book ends with the sad refrain, "In those days there was no king in Israel: every man did that which was right in his own eyes." A very sad period in the history of Israel.

At the end of this book, we come to the next book, Ruth, which begins with the words, "Now it came to pass in the days when the judges ruled," . . . "In those days there was a man whose name was Elimelech". (Ruth 1: 1, 2 NIV) During that period of time we are reminded that God still rules in Israel for there was a man whose name means "God is King" No matter what happens in the world, God is always King and His will is always working for the good of His people. Even though there was no king, the Lord was creating the circumstances from which His chosen King would come. This gives us a small insight into God's character, no matter how bad things seem to be, He is always concerned for the good of His people.

Elimelech lived in Bethlehemjudah but chose to leave his hometown because there was a famine in the Land. The Lord promised Israel that they would get their rain, at the proper time, if they would obey Him and if they did not the rain would not come. Even though there was a man whose name was “God is King”, the Land still suffered the consequences of the people’s disobedience. “Every man did what was right in his own eyes” and there was a famine in the Land. We have no indication as to what motivated Elimelech to leave with his family other than the fact that there was a famine in the Land.

Before long Elimelech died, away from his homeland and his two sons died after marrying Moabite girls; this left Naomi, Elimelech’s widow, living in a strange land with no relatives to support her, other than her two daughters in law. Israel had a system whereby people in need would be cared for by their families and Naomi decided to go back home where she would, at least, be among her relatives and she would benefit from the Israelite laws concerning widows. The Lord has a special compassion for the widow and the fatherless, people who are not able to help themselves.

One of the daughters in law, Orpah, decided to stay in Moab, her own land, while the other, Ruth, came back to Bethlehem with Naomi. Ruth learnt from Naomi’s example that her God was worth trusting so she committed herself to trusting the Lord and looked to Him for all her needs. As soon as these two widows returned to Naomi’s hometown we learn about one of Elimelech’s relatives, Boaz. In His wisdom, the Lord had designed the family for the protection of the individual. Herein lies the reason behind Naomi’s return to her homeland, she could expect her relatives to help her in her time of extreme need and, by the grace of God; she had at least one relative who was in a position to help her.

The Lord had given the Promised Land to Israel as a permanent possession as long as they were willing to obey His commandments. The Land was given to all of the people and divided among them according to their needs. Not only was the nation given the Land but every individual of the nation was given his own personal portion by right. Elimelech, Mahlon and Chilion had their own land in Bethlehemjudah.

While the Land was divided among the men, the women were given protection as well. If a woman was widowed without a son, who could own the land, then one of her husband's relatives was expected to take care of that problem so that she could still have access to the security of the land. This was an early system of social security that God had ordained so that the poor would be protected.

The book of Ruth is really just a commentary on this system that God had instituted in Israel, with the wonderful fruit of the kingly line being produced. Ruth was a poor woman who trusted in God, while Boaz was a relative of her husband's who also trusted in God. Ruth trusted in the Lord and followed the right procedures by claiming Boaz's protection, while Boaz was willing to accept his responsibility before the Lord.

God's Nature

The next question we need to consider is this: "What kind of God would even think about instituting such a system as this?"

It is part of human nature that we want to know where we come from. A child who is adopted will long to find out who their biological parents are so that they can know their true heritage. This occurs even though the adoptive parents are very good parents and the child has had all their other needs catered for in every possible way. God understood this need and, when He gave the Law to Moses, He began by telling Moses, and us, where we came from. The Bible begins, "In the beginning God . . ." (Genesis 1: 1) As soon as God begins to explain His relationship with the human race, He answers the question of our origin.

The first two words of the Bible contain the letters BRA, BRA. These two words are deliberately written in this way to show that "create" and "beginning" are mutually dependent. The word "create" can be explained by the word "beginning" and the word "beginning" can be explained by the word "create". This is the absolute beginning before which there was only God for it is only God who is able to create, man never creates in the way that God creates because he requires raw materials and then is able to form something from those raw materials. So we can form a picture of God when we look at the creative process. He is completely involved in the entire process but at every stage, when He creates, He brings new things into being, things that did not previously exist. This is a fundamental doctrine of the Old Testament, God was there before the beginning and, at the beginning, He made things that did not previously exist. This means that underlying everything else we have an absolute standard and God is not only the custodian of that standard, He is that standard. He is able to do everything and His only restrictions are those dictated by His love and His generosity. For example, He always remains true to His own loving and generous nature.

God introduces Himself at this stage with the name "Elohim" and when used in relationship with His capacity as creator this is entirely appropriate. This word is plural word and is a unique development of the Hebrew Scriptures that chiefly represents that fact that the Godhead is plural in terms of persons. This plurality also expresses the majesty and unity of God as the word is consistently used with singular verbs.

This God is the subject of all Divine activity as revealed to man and is the object of all true reverence and fear from man. God is absolute in every way and everything is under His absolute control. Nothing happens in the earth that is outside His will and nothing can ever happen that is outside His will. God is the supreme Ruler of the universe

This God, when He created, spoke His word and His word was fulfilled. There is no sense of struggle or hardship, when He created, if we can say this reverently, there was no sweat on His Divine brow - sweat on the brow is the fruit of sin - God's command comes and there is no possibility that the word will not be fulfilled. A recurring refrain is the fact that God said and it was so. So the God of the Old Testament is the God who is able to speak and there is nothing or no one who can prevent His commands from happening.

Furthermore, God is satisfied with what He has done. This is first indicated by the words, "And God saw the light that it was good" and finally summed up by the words, "And God saw every thing that he had made, and, behold, and it was very good." When God makes something it is good and He is always satisfied with the things that He has made.

God is the active God, Who does things and is distinct from the human race that He formed out of the dust of the earth. So we can answer the question, "Who is God?" with the answer, "He is the God Who acts" in the sense that He is distinct from us and far superior to us. For when we act or speak the consequences are sure but they are beyond our control while, for God, the consequences are always exactly as He envisages them.

Elohim, however, does not always exist in complete isolation. God is called by many names and even though He is distinct from His creation He is actively involved in the minute details of creation. He is known as "the God of heaven, which hath made the sea and the dry land." Our God does not need His creation but His creation needs Him.

God is also known by a group of names that express His sovereignty, the fact that He is Judge, eternal and the Saviour. God has an intimate and personal relationship with His people.

God is also known as "The LORD" and this name is written YHWH. The word is used with the pointing for the word "Adonay". LORD appears 6,828 times in the Bible and the word is only used in the Bible and nowhere else. It seems that Adam knew the Lord by this name for when his son Seth had a son called Enosh he began to formally worship the Lord. This name for God is His personal name that He chose to use in His covenant relationship with Israel. God formally made this covenant with Abraham and then introduced Himself to Moses using the same name when He met Moses in the burning bush.

The Lord exists and there is no question that He exists. When Moses asked God, "Suppose I go to the Israelites and say to them, 'The God of your fathers has sent me to you,' and they ask me, 'What is his name?' Then what shall I tell them?" God said to Moses, "'I AM WHO I AM.' This is what you are to say to the Israelites: 'I AM has sent me to you.'" (Exodus 3: 13, 14 NIV) When Moses asked the Lord for His name, he wanted to know something of the God's character and by giving this name to Moses the Lord defines His character and His relationship with His chosen people.

Not only does the Lord exist, He effects His will. For this is partly what He meant when He sent Moses with the command, "I AM hath sent me unto you." There is no question in the Lord's mind that this Name is sufficient to deliver Israel from slavery in Egypt and later to give them the Land that had been promised to them in the days of Abraham.

People today try to make arguments that prove the existence of God but with the Lord there is no need to prove that He exists. Just to mention His name, "I AM" is to acknowledge that He is there, He will always be there and He has always been there. The Lord has no need of any other person and is completely self-sufficient. He chooses to deal with man in His own way and man has no right to reach out to the Lord. In His own way and in His own time the Lord came to Moses and through Him to Israel but no one could force Him to act.

The Lord is the most powerful person in the entire universe and the name "I AM" assumes this without any question. He tells Moses, and us, that we can rely on Him and He is always consistent. When Abraham entertained the Lord and the Lord told him that He would soon have a son, Sarah laughed. Then the Lord said, "Is any thing too hard for the Lord?" (Genesis 18: 14 NIV) This question is always implied when the name of the Lord is used. The Lord God of the Old Testament is the One who can do all things and the One on whom we can always rely. He will never say one thing and do another. One of the most wonderful things about the Lord God is the fact that He can guarantee His word for there is no one who can stop Him doing what He makes up His mind to do.

So the Lord God of the Old Testament is all powerful and all knowing. No one can stay His hand or cause Him to change His mind. Now there are nine times in the Old Testament where it says that the Lord repented of something. This does not mean that the Lord changed His mind or demonstrated human frailty. He relents or changes his dealings with man according to His sovereign purposes. This is because, for time, judgment is conditional and a change in man's attitude can stay God's judgment.

While God remains absolute and powerful, He has the ability to relate to man in an intimate way and can hear the words of a single individual or one nation. So there are two dimensions of God in relation to man. Firstly, He is the great and Almighty God who controls all things and whose will is always done. While, secondly, He is the God who can be touched by the sorrow and pain of an individual and works to deal with their ways should they repent of their evil deeds.

It is in His capacity as the compassionate God of the individual in need in which the Lord commanded that the widow and the fatherless should be cared for He is loving and gracious and slow to anger. God will always care for His people when they cry out to Him in need. While they were slaves in Egypt, He delivered them and gave them a Land of their own. On their way out, He made sure that they did not leave empty handed. From that time forward, Israel were exhorted to remember that they had been slaves in Egypt and to moderate their behaviour towards the needy according to this fact.

Malachi is the last book of the Old Testament and the word Elohim is used 6 times while YHWH is used 46 times. God introduces Himself in Genesis as the Lord and the God and He remains the same right to the end of the Old Testament. He never changes and His character is always consistent, both in the Almighty and powerful dimension as well as the compassionate and personal dimension.

Yet Will I Hope In Him

When we have the God who is all powerful yet is interested in the needs of the weakest individual there is one proper response and that is to trust Him. For the outward expression of trust is obedience and obedience is the highest form of praise.

Broadly, two words are used to indicate trust in the Hebrew Bible. The first word has the synonyms: "safety", "confidence" and "security" when translated into English (batach). This word expresses the well known sense of security that comes from having someone to place confidence in. The Septuagint never translates this word with "believe in" but uses a word meaning "to hope" in the sense of "relying on God" or "to be persuaded" in the sense of relying on something that later proves to be deceptive. Here the sense does not indicate the full intellectual and emotional commitment that leads to faith but rather a feeling of being secure or safe. There is an ambivalent connotation when used of human relationships and often implies credulity or gullibility. The Old Testament contrasts that sense of confidence that comes from relying on God with the folly of relying on any other kind of security.

In pagan religions there is an unrequited anxiety while for the Hebrews there is the God Who is faithful and trustworthy, One on whom His people can rely with a confident expectation. The pagan always managed to find mechanisms whereby he could feel that he remained in control of his own destiny. On the other hand those who trust in God know that they are utterly without personal resources. It is, however, much better to be dependent on the gracious and dependable God than to be left to one's own devices in a world controlled by fickle and vindictive gods. The fact that God is sovereign and in complete control of man's destiny shows the futility of putting one's trust in any other person or thing. Trusting in God is not an automatic guarantee that a person will be insulated from hardship as God is always doing what is best for us rather than what we might want just now.

There are many sources of false security including: man, wickedness, violence and oppression, riches, and so on. In 2 Kings 18 and 19 the Assyrian Rabshakeh challenges the worth of Hezekiah's trust in God but that trust is later vindicated by God Himself.

The second word has the synonyms: "seek refuge", and "flee for protection" (hasah). This word is used literally in the sense of taking shelter from a rainstorm or fleeing to high hills for security from danger but more often it has the figurative sense of seeking refuge and thus putting confidence in any other god or in the shadow of a major power such as Egypt.

This idea of taking refuge may well derive from the common experience of fugitives or men at war for whom the adjacent hills provide a ready, safe height or strong rock to which a helpless person could flee for protection. Of course, the ultimate strong rock or safe height is the Lord Himself but when a person comes to Him they must come with an understanding of their own helplessness. It is always better to trust in God than in anything else because there is no one who is stronger than God. Who can come and plunder those who have taken security under His protection? This sense of helplessness emphasizes the defensive or external aspect of God's salvation.

God and man are contrasted in that God is able to do everything but man can only do things that the Lord allows. Our Lord is all powerful and knows everything but we are weak and restricted in our knowledge. There is only one proper response to God and that is to acknowledge our weakness and trust Him in everything we do. Naomi's situation began to improve the moment she returned to the shelter of the Almighty in Bethlehem. As long as she remained in Moab, she was dependent on the circumstances and the good will of the local people. Every good Israelite knew that the Lord had given them the Land and the Land was the place that they should be. As long as they trusted in the Lord and obeyed Him, He would protect them within the security of His strength.

Trusting God involves a simple acceptance that God is God and adapting our behaviour to that fact. If God is God, and He is, then surely His nature implies that we can rest secure in the safety of His generous love.

Substitution

Now, there seems to be two contradictory strands within the nature of God. On the one hand, He is the Holy God who does not tolerate sin while, on the other hand, He is concerned with the plight of the poor, helpless and downtrodden. How can God, for example, condemn Aaron's sons, Nadab and Abihu, to death while He was willing to pardon Rahab, the harlot, and absorb her into the Messianic line? The sons of Aaron burned unholy fire before the Lord but Rahab was a harlot and she lived in the land of Canaan that was devoted to destruction. Rahab placed her trust in the Lord while the other two men tried to do things their own way. Never the less, if God is God and sin is sin, then sin must be punished.

God has however instituted a way whereby sin may be expiated and throughout the history of Israel atonement has been available to sinners. They have been able to substitute the blood of another for their own sins.

The fact of substitution was best demonstrated during Abraham's life. For many years Abraham and Sarah longed to have a child. They could not have a child of their own and, at one stage, in a fit of despair; Sarah gave her husband one of her maids so that she could bear a child for her husband. But God is faithful and He had promised that Abraham and Sarah would have a son of their own. Well after Sarah had experienced menopause, she became pregnant and bore a son, whom they called Isaac, just as the Lord promised them. Some time later God tested Abraham and told him to go to a mountain and offer this special son as a sacrifice. We do not read anything about Abraham's feelings at that time but we do know that he did just as the Lord told him to do. At this stage Abraham believed that the Lord would bring his son back to life after he was killed on the altar. Even Isaac had to cooperate in this venture because he was strong enough to carry a bundle of wood on which the sacrifice would be burnt but he allowed his father, who was over a hundred years old, to tie him up and place him on the altar.

As Abraham, no doubt with a heavy heart, took the knife to kill his only son, the son for whom he had waited for so many years, an angel of the Lord called out to him from heaven. Abraham looked up and saw a ram caught nearby in a thicket. Now, while God had commanded Abraham to sacrifice his only son, God allowed a substitute for

Isaac. As far as Abraham was concerned, Isaac was already dead and all his actions led towards that end but God found a way to preserve Isaac and still allow the sacrifice to go ahead. Abraham told Isaac "God himself will provide the lamb for the burnt offering, my son." (Genesis 22: 8 NIV) At this stage it seemed as though God, for God had indeed provided the "lamb", had given this son to Abraham after so many years.

Even though God is absolutely holy and cannot abide sin, He allows sinners to take advantage of a substitute. To all intents and purposes, Isaac was dead but God rescued him. Sinners deserve to die but God allows them to take a substitute and kill the substitute in their place. When the Lord first instituted the Aaronic priesthood, He called upon the priests to come forward to be anointed and they were called upon to offer a bull. This bull was a sin offering, because the priests were only human and they had to make an offering for their own sin before they were anointed to this high and holy office before the Lord. By the grace of God, this substitute was accepted in their place and its life was taken in exchange for the lives of Aaron's family. This was not the only occasion when a substitute was given for the sins of the people, they were asked to offer a sin offering on the altar every day.

Once a year, on the great Day of Atonement, there was a grand substitution that took place. The high priest dressed in the robes of an ordinary priest in order to perform this duty. He would take two goat kids and sacrifice one. The other was called the scapegoat. During this ceremony, the priest placed his hands on the goat and it became a substitute for the nation. Their sins were placed on the goat and it was taken away into the desert and left there. In this way, the sins of the nation were taken away and sent into the desert in the form of their substitute.

The major problem with this form of substitution was that it had to take place on a continual basis. The substitutes could not do the job in a complete way because they were not of equal value with the people who committed the sins in the first place. They were able to be substitutes for a short time but as soon as there was sin again a new substitute had to be found in order to keep the people pure. As long as there were people alive in Israel there was a need for these sacrifices to take place until a better form of Substitute was found and this would only happen in the future.

When Israel first came out of slavery in Egypt there was a slightly different kind of substitution. All the firstborn males both of man and animal were killed in Egypt on the night of the first Passover. Israel, however, had a way of escaping from this terrible judgment; they were able to kill a lamb that was a year old and protect themselves by using its blood on around their doors on the outside. Whenever the angel saw that blood, he passed over that house and the firstborn were spared.

Later on the Lord told Israel that they would have to redeem the firstborn of animals and men because this had happened. Every firstborn male was saved from death by the substitution of the lamb in Egypt and from then on they were expected to redeem firstborn males. Because the firstborn males were spared, the Lord claimed the tribe of Levi for His own. Moses was asked to number the firstborn males in Israel and to number the men in the tribe Levi and then he had to pay a ransom because there were more firstborn than there were Levites.

This establishes a further principle that substitution is related to redemption. When one person is liable for a debt, another person can redeem the debt for them hence becoming their substitute.

Redemption

The Hebrew Bible uses three synonyms for the concept of redemption (ga'al, padah and kapar). Originally these words were used with similar meanings but, with time, they developed slightly different technical senses.

"Kapar" was a word that was used, in a technical sense, in relation to Israel's sacrificial rituals and on the simplest level means a material transaction or a ransom. There was a time when David was concerned that there was a famine in Israel that lasted for three years. David asked the Lord what the problem was and he discovered that the former king Saul had killed some of the Gibeonites even though Joshua had made a covenant with them many years before. David said to the Gibeonites, “What shall I do for you? How shall I make amends so that you will bless the Lord’s inheritance?” (2 Samuel 21: 3 NIV) In this case David wanted to know what price was required to make amends, that is, to ransom or redeem Israel from the bloodguilt incurred by Saul. They required that some of Saul’s descendants be killed as the price of redemption.

Sometimes God, Himself is called upon to pay the price of redemption. In the days when Hezekiah was king, the Passover was held and some people did not purify themselves according to the correct rituals and then they took the Passover. Now according to the Law these people should have died “But Hezekiah prayed for them, saying, ‘May the LORD, who is good, pardon everyone.’” (2 Chronicles 30: 18 NIV) In this case the Lord, Himself, was asked to atone for their sins, that is, He was asked to pay the price of their redemption for they should have died.

The most frequent use of this word has to do with specific rites and the priest is the one who makes atonement on behalf of the people. Blood always plays a prominent part in the process of atonement. That is, in the sacrifices associated with atonement it is necessary for blood to be shed to pay the price of redemption.

This word is used in modern day Hebrew, as well in the classical times, in the term “Yom Kippur” which is the term used to describe the Day of Atonement when the scapegoat was sent away as a substitute for the people. Sometimes this word is also translated as “propitiate” or “expiate” where expiate has God as the subject and propitiate has God as the object of the atonement. In the end, however, all the animal sacrifices in the world would not be sufficient to satisfy the righteous judgment of Almighty God and

God alone can provide the atonement that will satisfy His wrath. Real redemption can only come from God. The Pharisees backed up this statement when they said, "Who can forgive sins but God alone?" (Mark 2: 7 NIV)

"Padah" has the basic meaning of achieving a change of ownership through the payment of a price or exchanging an equivalent substitute. In the early times this was actually used for a commercial transaction.

A slave girl can be redeemed if a man deals with in her a treacherous way. If a man takes a girl in order to marry her but later he breaks this promise then the girl must not be sold to a strange nation but he must allow her to be redeemed because he was not honest in his own dealings with the girl. In this case the man must bear the price of redemption because of his own sin.

During the time of King Saul, the Israelites were in battle and the king said that anyone who ate food before the Philistines were conquered would die. Jonathan, Saul's son, did not hear the prohibition and ate some honey later he was condemned to death but the people rescued (redeemed) Jonathan and he did not die. This was another case of someone being rescued from certain death. This is the word that was used in relation to the Exodus. Israel was redeemed from bondage in Egypt; later in the history of Israel this God who had redeemed them from bondage in Egypt was able to redeem them from all adversity.

The third word, "Ga'al" is used primarily in relation to the duty of the relative. When a person found themselves in difficulty or danger then their relative had a duty to redeem his kin from the problems. Redemption is seen as the privilege as well as the duty of the relative. There are four basic things that a honest and reliable man would do for his relative. Firstly he should be prepared to redeem property when the owner finds himself in a time of adversity and has to sell the land or relative has to sell himself into slavery in order to pay off debts or obligations. In the second case there was the redemption of property or non sacrificial animals that had been dedicated to the Lord, such as the first born of an unclean animal. In this case an equivalent amount was to be given then an extra amount was to be added to avoid any possibility of dishonesty. Thirdly the root of this word is used for the avenger of blood when a murder was committed. In this case the next of kin was to effect the payment of a life for a life. Lastly in the Psalms and the prophets there is the idea that God is Israel's Redeemer, He will stand up for His people and vindicate them. There may be a hint of the Father's near kinship or ownership in the use of this word.

Kinsman

The next logical step at this stage is to examine the concept of the kinsman. There are three words that are translated "kinsman" in the King James Version of the Old Testament.

In the book of Ruth, Boaz is described as the kinsman of Ruth and the word used in this case is "moda" the same word is used in Proverbs in a figurative sense, "Say to wisdom, 'You are my sister' and call understanding your kinsman." (Proverbs 7: 4 NIV) The root word behind this is the word "yada" which means, "to know", the root of this word occurs 944 times in the Old Testament and expresses a multitude of shades of knowledge gained by the senses.

God knows men and their ways and this knowledge begins before they are born. The word can also be used of men's knowledge and for that of animals. When the participle is used this word can mean skill at hunting, learning, sailing the seas or playing an instrument. Sometimes it can mean to distinguish between good and evil, which was the result of man's first act of disobedience against God.

This word can also be used of acquaintance between people. When Abraham's servant returned to Haran to find a wife for Isaac, he asked the local people, "Do you know Laban?" (Genesis 29: 5 NIV) In this case he was asking the local people if they were acquainted with Laban rather than if they were his relatives. On the other hand, the word may mean relative. When Jehu took the kingdom away from Ahab he killed all his relatives as well. This was to ensure that there was no one else alive who might try to claim a legitimate right to the throne that he had so recently taken for himself.

Moses was a very special man and He had a special relationship with God because we read of Moses that he knew God face to face and that God knew him by name. We can also speak of the most intimate form of knowing as in the euphemism, "Adam knew his wife Eve." This word can also be used of one's relationship with foreign gods or with the Lord Himself. The plagues that the Lord sent to Egypt were sent so that they might know that the Lord is God. Ezekiel prophesied against a sinful Israel and many of his prophecies were made so that "you will know that I am the LORD." (Ezekiel 6: 7 NIV)

We could well conclude from the use of this word that the Lord, Himself, was the kinsman of Israel because He knew them in the most intimate and complete way.

Another word used to indicate kinsman comes from the root word "qarab" meaning "I come near" or "enter into". The root word means "being in" or "coming into" near and intimate proximity with the subject or the object. It can also mean actual contact with another person or object.

The adjective "qarob" can indicate nearness in time, space, family ties or interest. So from this we have the word "kinsman" someone who is near to a person in family ties. This sense of kinsman can also be used to show that the Lord has a special relationship of kinship with Israel for He is always near them. When they travelled in the wilderness, the Lord went before them to lead them and went behind them to protect them. Every time they stayed the Lord stayed with them. His nearness was always seen in the pillar of cloud or of fire by day or by night.

Lastly the word used for "redeemer" (ga'al) can also be used as "kinsman". A kinsman is not only someone who knows us and is near to us but this person also has a responsibility to us as we have a responsibility towards our kin. In modern, industrialized, urbanized society the concept of kin is not so important. There are many people who care for their relatives but there are many others who feel no obligation to them at all. How many older people are put away in homes so that they are not a burden to their families? It would be hard to number the rich or comfortable people who have poor relatives.

God is not only the Kinsman, in every sense, of Israel but He is also our Kinsman because He knows all about us and He is always near us and he cares for us when we need Him. He even cares for us when we are not willing to recognize that we need help at all

The Early Promise

When Noah came out of the ark, he was in a kinsman relationship with God for he was near to God and he knew God. The Lord spoke to Noah and he obeyed, spending many years building an ark even though there had not been any rain on the earth and the concept of a flood was entirely alien to his mind. He knew that the Lord was God and that he had an obligation to obey the Lord so he did what he was told even though it took many years to build the ark. In this way, we can see that Noah understood that God was close to Him because he heard the Lord's voice and he did what he was told. We can believe, too, that Noah knew the Lord because if he did not know the Lord then how would he know to obey him? A ga'al relationship existed as well because the Lord took upon Himself the obligation of delivering Noah from certain death by giving the instructions to build the ark and then closing the door behind him before the rain started.

After the time of Noah, there is no evidence that his descendants actually continued in their relationship as God's kinsmen for we do not read of people who knew the Lord or appreciated His close presence. God, however, did not forget that He loved the earth and was willing to keep her people under the security of His protection.

As far as we know, Abram did not know God in any way before God called him. He lived in Ur of the Chaldees with his father Nahor and then the whole family moved to Haran. While they were living there, Abram, who we assume was an idolater, like everyone else at the time, heard the Lord telling him to leave his home and go away to a Land that would be shown to him. Now here is the embryo of a kinsman relationship. Abram knew the Lord because he heard His voice and He recognized that this was the God Who must be obeyed for he obeyed Him. Not only did Abram know the Lord but there was a strong sense of His being near and even an understanding of an obligation to care. The Lord did say, "Leave your country, your people and your father's household and go to the Land I will show you. I will make you into a great nation and I will bless you; I will make your name great, and you will be a blessing. I will bless those who bless you, and whoever curses you I will curse; and all the families on earth will be blessed through you." (Genesis 12: 1-3 NIV)

As time went by Abram became Abraham and he was know as the friend of God. God, however, had other plans that were soon to be revealed. God made a binding covenant with Abraham. There was an ancient custom when a covenant or contract was made where an animal was killed and then cut in half. When the pieces were laid on the ground the two parties making the covenant walked between the halves of the animal and then the covenant was legally binding. As God made the covenant with Abraham, He walked among the animals by Himself so becoming kinsman (ga'al) Himself by taking the obligation Himself

When God made His covenant with Abram, He asked Abram to take one of every species which was allowed or commanded to be sacrificed in the Mosaic Law and kill them and cut the pieces in half and lay them on the ground. When the sun had set Abram fell asleep and then he saw smoking furnace and a burning lamp pass between the halves of the carcasses. The Lord promised Abram that He would bless him and his descendants and through him all the families of the earth would be blessed. Now, an interesting thing about this covenant is that God made the covenant binding on Himself but He did not call upon Abram to walk between the divided carcasses.

As God made His binding covenant with Abram, soon to be Abraham, He accepted an obligation Himself without forcing Abram to accept any obligation. At this stage God chose to take the role of Kinsman on Abraham's behalf but, as Abram had nothing to offer God except faith, Abraham was cast in the role of person in need. This relationship continues in one way or another throughout the rest of the Old Testament and down on into the New Testament.

When the Israelites were slaves in Egypt their Kinsman was ready to help them and to take them into their own Land. One might ask, "Why did the Lord allow them to wait so long in Egypt and suffer the degradation of slavery?" Well the Lord has knowledge and wisdom which is far superior to ours and He knew exactly what was needed to make Israel into a cohesive nation that would be able to carry out His larger plan of bringing blessing to all the families of the earth.

After God delivered Israel from slavery in Egypt, He gave them the Law at Sinai. This Law did not undo the earlier promise or remove God's acceptance of the ga'al responsibility. God specially chose Israel as His own nation and delivered them from slavery before they were given the Law. Their Kinsman had already taken his responsibility and now they belonged to Him. There is a great responsibility that belongs to people who are known as the people of God. The Lord was giving Canaan to the Israelites because He had previously promised the Land to them but they were acting as agents of the Lord's justice as well. Canaan had become the home of a morally degenerate people who were idolaters and extremely wicked.

The Law was given to Israel to show them how they should live as the people of God. Not only is it a great honour to be the people of God; there is a responsibility as well. If the Canaanites were driven out of their land because of their moral degeneracy then God's people had an obligation to remain separate from that degeneracy. The Law told the people that they had to be responsible and they had to live in a way that honoured God or they would suffer the same fate as their predecessors. It did not undo the kinsman relationship that God had established with Abraham and his descendants but reminded them of their privilege and its accompanying responsibility.

Their obedience would also be the means whereby God drew other people to Himself and so blessed all the families of the earth.

The Promise Renewed

Just before the Israelites went into the land of Canaan they were faced with a crisis. Ever since they were slaves in Egypt Moses had been their leader. He was the man chosen and equipped by God to lead them out of slavery. If Moses had not come on the scene they would probably have ceased to exist as a nation in a very short time and passed into history as a forgotten and forgettable people. Pharaoh commanded that all the male Hebrew children be killed as soon as they were born. However, apart from three men, all those who were slaves in Egypt were dead and all the younger people knew nothing other than Moses as leader.

Moses was not going to cross the Jordan. Even though Joshua had been Moses' servant for many years, he was untried as a leader. Certain questions were being asked. Would the promise of the Land continue now that Moses the servant of the Lord was no longer there to lead them? After all, Moses was the man who met the Lord in the burning bush and he was the man who, under God's authority, challenged Pharaoh and eventually led the slaves to freedom.

As the people waited on the banks of the Jordan, the Lord confirmed the covenant that He previously made with Abraham. They were told that the title deeds of the Land belonged to them, the Land which had been promised and in which their fathers had lived as strangers. Even though the Law contained clauses about obedience and the consequences of not obeying, the covenant still stood. There was always the, "If you repent" clause. As long as Israel repented they would be brought back to the Land and they would own it again. People who live in the last half of the twentieth century will know that the Lord keeps His word because we have seen the Jews return to their homeland after one of the great madmen of the century tried to kill every Jew on the face of the earth.

There were two portions of the covenant that God made with Abraham, the first part related to the Land but the second part related to his seed. We read in the New Testament that Abraham's seed is a single person, the Lord Jesus Christ. This seed was to come through Judah, from whom the sceptre was not to depart. Israel was designed as a constitutional monarchy. At the time they entered the Land they needed to have a strong and experienced general as their leader and the Lord gave them the right man for this job.

Eventually God brought Israel to the time when they were ready to have their own king. Before they had the king of God's choice, they had a king of their own choice and this was to prove detrimental to their well being in the short term but God was using this experience to prepare them properly for their rightful king. Without Saul, all of Israel would not have followed David with such devotion. The Lord, however, renewed the covenant again in relation to their king.

David took some time to establish himself as king, after the death of Saul. There were still people in Israel who wanted to have Saul's descendants as their king and, for a time, there were two kings in the Land. When David was finally established, he decided that it was time for him to build a Temple for the Lord. He asked Nathan if he should do so and Nathan told him to go ahead. Later the Lord told Nathan that David could not build the Temple because he had blood on his hands. At this stage, the Lord made a covenant with David, "Your house and your kingdom will endure forever before me; your throne will be established forever." (2 Samuel 7: 16) This was not a new covenant but another renewal of the old covenant that was made to Abraham. There is even a hint of this covenant at the very beginning of the reign of sin on the earth.

The covenant that God made with David was unconditional; there would always be a descendant of David alive to claim the throne. In the New Testament we see the absolute fulfilment of this promise when the greatest of all David's descendants rose from the dead and returned to rule in heaven. In eternity David's greatest descendant will rule forever. There would be times when a particular descendant of David did not sit on the throne and that was because that man or some of his predecessors sinned and were not worthy to sit on the throne. In the final case, the descendant will sit on the throne of the entire earth and through that will also reign in Israel.

Time and again as we move through the Old Testament, the Lord makes covenants with Israel and in each case the covenant is based on the first one with Abraham that includes the words, "and through your offspring all nations on earth will be blessed, because you have obeyed me." (Genesis 22: 18 NIV) The promise is always an eternal and unconditional covenant that relies on the faithfulness and might of Almighty God.

A Massive Failure

David's son, Solomon, became king and he asked the Lord to give him "a discerning heart to govern your people and to distinguish between right and wrong" (1 Kings 3: 9 NIV). However before long this Solomon showed a lack of faith and began to make political alliances with the nations around him by marrying foreign women and they led his heart astray from the Lord. So the kingly line began to decline and David's grandson, Rehoboam lost the United Kingdom and only ruled over the tribes of Judah and Benjamin with the tribe f Levi associated with the Temple.

It is important to distinguish between the covenant that the Lord made with Abraham, renewed just before the people crossed the river Jordan and updated with David when he sought to build the Temple and the Law. When the Lord made His covenant with Abraham, it was an unconditional covenant and the Lord, Himself, guaranteed that this covenant would be kept. On the other hand the Law stipulated that the people needed to keep certain commandments and obligations so that the rain would come and they would remain in the Land the Lord gave them when they came out of bondage. One covenant was a covenant of permanent blessing while the other covenant was one of current tenure in the Land.

The Lord, in His infinite wisdom, told the Israelites that they had to respect the Land and to give it time to recover so that it could maintain its productivity. In order to do this the Land was to be given Sabbaths every seven years where it was not cultivated. On top of this there was to be the year of Jubilee every fiftieth year where the land was given an extra year to recover. No one was allowed to take the produce of the land and they were to allow anything that grew to rot and go back to the earth.

Now the kingdom of Judah chose not to obey this ruling after they separated from the ten northern tribes. While Israel, or Ephraim as they are sometimes called, sinned in the same way as the Canaanites and were removed from the Land because they made their own idols so that they people would not go back to Jerusalem for the Temple. However, before they were taken away there was a Passover held in Hezekiah's time and believing people from every tribe came down to Judah so they were not taken away into exile and every tribe was represented in the remnant in Judah.

In the mean time Judah maintained the Temple for most of the time and followed some form of godly worship there. Except for a short interregnum during the time of Athaliah; a son of David remained on the throne until Nebuchadnezzar finally sacked Jerusalem. After that, however, Jehoiachin was raised to a position of favor in Babylon and lived the remainder of his life as a king in captivity. The Lord was not pleased with Judah and they were punished for their sins. Jeremiah told them that they would be taken away as captives for seventy years so that the land could have its Sabbaths and recuperate from the years where it was given no rest. This did not however abrogate the covenant that God made with Abraham because even though most of the people from the kingdom of Judah were not in the Land the Lord did tell them, "When seventy years are completed for Babylon, I will come to you and fulfil my gracious promise to bring you back to this place. For I know the plans I have for you, . . . plans to prosper you and not to harm you, plans to give you hope and a future. Then you will call upon me and come and pray to me, and I will listen to you. You will seek me and find me when you seek me with all your heart. I will be found by you . . . and will bring you back from captivity. I will gather you from all the nations and places where I have banished you, and will bring you back to the place from which I carried you into exile." (Jeremiah 29: 10-14) The promise of the Land and the kinsman relationship that the Lord first established with Abraham still remained and would never be broken. Just because the people were not living in the way that was appropriate, for those who belonged to the Lord, He did not change His own nature or become unfaithful to His promises. Judah failed the Lord but the Lord did not fail Judah. They may have gone into captivity in Babylon but they went into that captivity with a promise that they would return and the Land would belong to them once more.

The Redeemer Acts

Nebuchadnezzar did not completely conquer Judah in one attack. The chronology was as follows. Hezekiah lived between approximately 770 and 690 BC. At one stage in his reign this king was almost dead but he asked the Lord to spare his life and he lived and extra fifteen years. During these extra fifteen years, Hezekiah showed off his wealth to messengers sent by Berodachbaladan, the son of Baladan, king of Babylon. Isaiah the prophet told Hezekiah that all the wealth he had shown to the messengers of the Babylon's king would one day be taken away to Babylon.

Hezekiah had a very evil son called Manasseh who led his people far away from the high standards that were set for them as God's people. Manasseh was succeeded by Amon who was killed by some of his servants and then the good king Josiah ruled in Judah. At the end of Josiah life he interfered in a battle between Egypt and Syria and was killed by Paroahnechoh. Josiah's son Jehoahaz was anointed king but Pharaoh came and deposed this king and replaced him with his brother Jehoiakim. Nebuchadnezzar attacked Jehoiakim and made his a vassal but Jehoiakim rebelled after three years. Jehoiakim died and his son Jehoiachin reigned in his place. At this stage Nebuchadnezzar comprehensively defeated the Egyptians. Nebuchadnezzar then attacked Jerusalem and took the king away and many of leading people, leading them captive in Babylon. Isaiah's prophecy was fulfilled and all the treasures were taken to Babylon. The Babylonians now appointed Zedekiah as vassal king. In the ninth year of Zedekiah's reign the Babylonians came and set a siege against Jerusalem, the siege remained until the eleventh year of Zedekiah's reign when the Babylonians broke through and the city and the Temple were destroyed. All of Zedekiah's sons were killed and his eyes were put out before he was taken captive to Babylon. Some poor people were left behind but the nation of Judah no longer existed. They were now absorbed into the Babylonian Empire and no longer had possession of the Land that the Lord had given them.

Judah had lost possession of their Land because they did not live in the way that God prescribed. They were God's chosen people and they had a responsibility to live according to their high calling. However God had made a permanent covenant with Abraham and God had taken upon Himself the responsibility of being Judah's Kinsman.

We have seen earlier that Jeremiah prophesied that they would return to their Land seventy years later.

As far as the rest of the world was concerned, Judah no longer existed as a nation. They had neither the resources nor the manpower to take possession of the Land again; their situation was completely hopeless. Yet after the seventy years had elapsed their Redeemer acted as Kinsman. Darius the Median defeated Babylon. During the reign of Cyrus king of Persia, Israel's Redeemer acted and they returned to their Land with a royal warrant to rebuild the walls of their city and the Temple. All the wealth that had been stolen from the Temple by the Babylonians was returned to Jerusalem in a miraculous way. The Lord did not forget His eternal covenant and He acted when it was impossible for anyone else to act.

Hopelessness

An important aspect of redemption was the fact that the value of the person or thing being redeemed should not be underestimated. It was not proper that someone pay a small price to redeem land or livestock when the price should be large. In fact, when people made vows to the Lord then the value was stipulated in the Law. No one was allowed to alter the value that was set by the priest and no one was allowed to substitute a good beast for a bad beast or a bad beast for a good beast. If a man wanted to redeem an animal or some land, he would add a fifth to the value estimated by the priest and then he would pay that price. This was to make sure that there was no underhand dealing and that the full price of redemption was paid.

When King David numbered Israel against God's wishes, God offered him a choice of what punishment he wanted. As the punishment proceeded, David reached the stage where he saw an angel ready to strike Jerusalem and then the plague was averted. King David decided that he would buy the threshing floor that belonged to Araunah and Araunah offered to give him the land. David refused to accept the gift and said, "I will not sacrifice to the LORD my God burnt offerings that cost me nothing" (2 Samuel 24: 24 NIV) to use a modern phrase, "there is no such thing as getting something for nothing".

We have seen earlier that Israel had to redeem their firstborn when they came out of Egypt as payment for the fact that the angel did not kill their firstborn. The Lord took the tribe of Levi to be His own in exchange for the firstborn of Israel and extra money had to be paid to complete the price of redemption as there were more firstborn than men in the tribe of Levi.

Abraham spent some time bargaining with the Lord over the fate of Sodom. His nephew Lot lived there and Abraham hoped to save the city from destruction. During this episode, Abraham negotiated with the Lord to spare the city. He began by asking for fifty righteous men and went down to asking if the city could be spared for the sake of ten righteous men. While the discussion continued, Abraham stated his justification for continuing this negotiation using the words, "Will not the Judge of all the earth do right?" (Genesis 18: 25 NIV) This means that it is right before God that proper value be given when there is redemption.

During the first period Moses spent on Mount Sinai with the Lord receiving the Law, the Israelites sinned and made a golden calf saying that this idol was the God Who had delivered them from slavery. The Lord was angry with Israel and threatened to destroy them and Moses asked the Lord if he could become their substitute. He said, "'But now, please forgive their sin - but if not, then blot me out of the book you have written.' The LORD replied to Moses, 'Whoever has sinned against me I will blot out of my book.'" (Exodus 32: 32-33 NIV) In this case there was not proper value for the substitution. While Moses was the friend of God, he did sin in his own right and was forbidden entry into the Promised Land for his sin.

Ezekiel wrote about Noah, Daniel, and Job. The Lord told him about Israel's idolatry and how they had become estranged from God through their idolatry. They were urged to repent and to turn away from their idols and all the associated practices. When sin was so bad in the Land there was only one option that the Lord could take and that was to punish the people and destroy the Land. God goes on to say, "even if these three men - Noah, Daniel and Job - were in it, they could save only themselves by their righteousness, declares the Sovereign LORD." (Ezekiel 14: 14 NIV) This idea is repeated three times throughout the passage.

Noah was a righteous man who obeyed God and built the ark when he was told to do so. But even for all his righteousness and the fact that God saved him from the flood, Noah would only be able to save himself and no one else. Job was a man of great patience who trusted the Lord and eventually spoke with the Lord but he would not be good enough to redeem another person through his own righteousness. Daniel was a great leader in Babylon and, no doubt, was well known among the exiles for his prominent role in that kingdom. God spoke with Daniel and gave him the true meaning of some special dreams but even Daniel would not be able to redeem another person by his goodness.

Israel could only look to the Lord as their Redeemer because, even among all the great men and women of faith, there was no person who was able to redeem them. God looks for value when He accepts a redeemer and the payment of the price of redemption but any one person only has the value of one person and their faith is only sufficient to be counted for their own salvation if for anyone at all. After spending their time in captivity in Babylon, Israel could only look to the Lord for redemption so that they could return to the Land.

Future Promise

Even while Israel was sinning and experiencing their worst setback in the Old Testament period, the Lord was still reaffirming His original, unconditional covenant. The Lord was telling Israel that, even though they could not find a redeemer from among all of their great men and women, He was their Kinsman and He would pay the price of their redemption Himself. He is the only person who is of sufficient value to satisfy the demands of redemption.

Ezekiel reaffirmed the Lord's promise, "Yet I will remember the covenant I made with you in the days of your youth, and I will establish an everlasting covenant with you.

Then you will remember your ways and be ashamed when you receive your sisters, both those who are older than you and those who are younger. I will give them to you as daughters, but not on the basis of my covenant with you. So I will establish my covenant with you, and you will know that I am the LORD." (Ezekiel 16: 60-62) The despair of knowing that the best of their heroes is unable to redeem any other person is mitigated by the hope that God Himself is their Kinsman.

Jeremiah gives a new covenant from the Lord, "'The time is coming,' declares the LORD, 'when I will make a new covenant with the house of Israel and with the house of Judah. It will not be like the covenant I made with their forefathers when I took them by the hand to lead them out of Egypt, because they broke my covenant, though I was a husband to them' declares the LORD. 'This is the covenant I will make with the house of Israel after that time,' declares the LORD. 'I will put my law in their minds and write it on their hearts. I will be their God, and they will be my people. No longer will a man teach his neighbour, or a man his brother, saying, "Know the LORD," because they will all know me, from the least of them to the greatest.' declares the LORD. 'For I will forgive their wickedness and will remember their sins no more.'" (Jeremiah 31: 31-34) This new covenant is even better than the old one for it will exist in their hearts and not be a matter of external ceremony

Better that all of this is the promise that there will, one day, be a Hero of Israel Who by His own goodness will be able to redeem the rest of His people. This Person is the suffering servant of Isaiah. It is said of Him, "Yet it was the Lord's will to crush him and cause him to suffer, and though the LORD makes his life a guilt offering, he will see his offspring and prolong his days, and the will of the LORD will prosper in his hand. After the suffering of his soul, he will see the light of life and be satisfied; by his knowledge my righteous servant will justify many, and he will bear their iniquities. Therefore I will give him a portion among the great, and he will divide the spoils with the strong, because he poured out his life unto death, and was numbered with the transgressors. For he bore the sin of many, and made intercession for the transgressors." (Isaiah 53: 10-12 NIV) The Old Testament looked forward to this Man who would be able to justify many and not just Himself. This man will be satisfied because He was able to bear the iniquities of His people. He will be satisfied because, as their Kinsman, He has paid the full price of redemption. The Judge of all the earth will do right and the price of redemption will be paid in full value.

God chose Israel, not because they had anything to offer Him, because He had many good things to give them and so that, through their existence, He would find a way of blessing all the families of the earth. Sometimes a person becomes a kinsman through the biological process of birth but at other times a person becomes a kinsman by adoption. The Lord adopted Abraham and promised Abraham that He would be Kinsman to Abraham and his seed. In a similar way, the Lord has adopted all the people of the earth who trust in the Lord Jesus Christ as their own personal Saviour and He has made Himself our Kinsman.

No One Is Good - Except God Alone

The English versions of the Old Testament end with the promise of a curse. “See, I will send you the prophet Elijah before that great and dreadful day of the LORD comes. He will turn the hearts of the fathers to their children, and the hearts of the children to their fathers; or else I will come and strike the land with a curse.” (Malachi 4: 5, 6 NIV) There is also a promise that the prophet Elijah will come.

As a general rule, we do not read birth notices in the press of men or women who are going to be famous. When a king, a prime minister or a president has a child, the media may note the event. Some people may try to predict that this child will do certain things but no one can know for certain. However, at their death all the good or bad things they have done can be documented with certainty.

The Old Testament, on the other hand, has the pleasant fragrance of Someone special Who is going to come and He will restore all things so that the Lord's people will know the Lord again. This special Person is known as the Messiah and when He comes to rule, as the righteous Prince, there will be righteousness on the earth. There is a sense of inevitability about the coming of the Messiah and what He will do on the earth. This Man will deliver Israel and all the nations of the earth from sin. Before His birth, it was said of Him, "you are to give him the name Jesus, because he will save his people from their sins." (Matthew 1: 21 NIV) This prophecy was exactly correct.

First in Prophecy

As soon as sin entered the world, the Lord promised that Eve's seed would one day crush the serpent's head. While this prophecy indicates that there will be perpetual warfare between the woman's descendants and the serpent it does allow for the fact that the entire family of humanity may be represented by one individual who will finally and definitively crush the head of the serpent C F Kiel and F Delitzsch have this to say about this individual: "The question, therefore, who is to be understood by the 'seed' which is to crush the serpent's head, can only be answered from the history of the human race. But a point of much greater importance comes into consideration here. Against the natural serpent the conflict may be carried on by the whole human race, by all who are born of the woman, but not against Satan. As he is a foe who can only be met with spiritual weapons, none can encounter him successfully but such as possess and make use of spiritual arms. Hence the idea of the 'seed' is modified by the nature of the foe. If we look at the natural development of the human race, Eve bore three sons but only one of them, namely, Seth was really the seed by whom the human family was preserved through the flood and perpetuated in Noah: so, again, of the three sons of Noah, Shem, the blessed of Jehovah, from whom Abraham descended was the only one in whose seed all the nations were to be blessed, and that not through Ishmael, but through Isaac alone. Through these constantly repeated acts of divine selection, which were not arbitrary exclusions, but were rendered necessary by differences in the spiritual condition of the individuals concerned. The 'seed' to which the victory over Satan was promised, was spiritually or ethically determined, and ceased to be co-extensive with physical descent. This spiritual seed culminated in Christ, in whom the Adamite family terminated, henceforward to be renewed by Christ as the second Adam, and restored by him to its original exaltation and likeness to God. In this sense, Christ is the seed of the woman who tramples Satan under his feet, not as an individual, but as the head both of the posterity of the woman which kept the promise and maintained the conflict with the old serpent before His advent, and also of those who are gathered out of all nations, are united to Him by faith and formed into one body of which His is the head." (This is a quote from the *Commentary on the Old Testament in Ten volumes*, by C F Kiel and F Delitzsch, translated by James Martin, volume 1, published by William B Eerdmans Publishing Company, Grand Rapids, Michigan, 1980, pages 101-102)

On the first day that there was sin in the world, the Lord cursed the sinners and then He promised that one day sin would be overcome and the relationship would be restored. The curse was not a prophecy but the promise of the seed Who would trample the serpent's head. So the story of salvation began with the promise of a Saviour. Our Saviour was both the object and the subject of this promise.

We read that the "Word", Christ Jesus, our Saviour is God, and it was God who promised that the Seed would come to conquer, while at the same time He fought with Satan and crushed his head at Calvary.

Paul, the apostle, tells us that the Lord Jesus Christ is the "seed" of Abraham as promised by the Lord when He first made His covenant with Abraham. In this sense, all the prophecies relating to the Messiah in the Old Testament are founded on this the first promise. In fact, the whole of the Old Testament becomes a book that points to Christ and tells us that we need Him and without Him the serpent will always conquer.

Our Saviour, Christ Jesus, is the first among all the people whose lives were foretold, there are more prophecies about Him in the Old Testament than any other person. If scholars of His day had taken the time to investigate the prophets, especially Daniel, they could easily have determined that He was the only person who could satisfy all the prophecies about the Messiah.

First In Having A Forerunner

Even though the entire Old Testament is about preparing for the coming of the Messiah and proof that He is absolutely essential for any kind of genuine salvation, there are prophecies concerning other people and other events. One of these other people is the forerunner. Before the Lord Jesus could come to the earth it was necessary that someone else come before Him to prepare the way for Him. Sometimes a great king, president or general may send envoys ahead of him so that all will be ready for his coming but no one, apart from our Redeemer, had someone sent before he was born so that they could prepare the way for his coming.

John the Baptist appeared preaching a baptism of repentance. He was a man of great reputation and many of the leaders of his day tried to find out about him. John explained that he was not a special person himself but there was Someone Who was coming, Who was special. John proclaimed that the One who was coming would be able to baptise with the Holy Ghost.

Part of the reason for John the Baptist's coming goes back to Genesis chapter 3. We saw earlier that out of the "Fall" came the promise of reconciliation and someone who would be able to bring about that reconciliation. After Adam and Eve took the fruit, they heard the Lord walking in the garden. Now, it seems that it was the habit of the Lord to walk in the garden so that Adam and Eve could enjoy His love. There is also no indication that sin was in the world for long ages before the serpent came to tempt Adam and Eve. It is quite possible that the angels were created during the course of the six creative days and God left that fact out of the record because it was not essential to the story of the beginning, as far as the Israelites were concerned. Perhaps Satan sinned and the great spiritual battle took place earlier on the same day he came to tempt Adam and Eve.

After our first ancestors succumbed to the temptation, the Lord came and called for them in the garden. Now the Lord already knew that they had sinned so why did He call to them in the garden? He walked in the garden to give them a chance to repent. They had the choice of coming straight to the Lord and telling Him that they had chosen to disobey and had eaten the fruit but they hid. Instead of owning their sin, Eve blamed the serpent and Adam blamed Eve.

When John the Baptist appeared, he preached repentance. Repentance involves a person changing their mind, and in the New Testament, always changing it for the better and there should be a sense of regret for past behaviour. When Adam and Eve had the opportunity to repent they did not take it and so they chose to cut themselves off from God.

Their temptation was, "you will be like God." (Genesis 3: 5 NIV) In essence that is what sinners choose to do. It is a very pleasant thought for a person to imagine that they will be in complete control of their lives. The Lord Jesus Christ came to restore the relationship between God and man but first there had to be repentance. There is no room for more than one God on the earth. While we know that there is only one God, many people assume that they can take the place of God in their own lives. Our Saviour came to this earth to restore the relationship, which previously existed between God and man, but first we have to show a genuine sense of sorrow for previously trying to take the place of God ourselves. No one else in history required a forerunner to prepare people for His coming. No one was as holy as the Lord that genuine repentance was required as a basis for any relationship between God and man. The Lord Jesus Christ is outstanding in history in so far as someone needed to come and preach repentance so that the world would be ready for Him to come.

First In God's Eternal Purposes

The book of Hebrews begins with a remarkable statement, "In the past God spoke to our forefathers through the prophets at many times and in various ways, but in these last days he has spoken to us by his Son, whom he appointed heir of all things." (Hebrews 1: 1, 2 NIV) Even though Paul rejoiced in the fact that he was the apostle to the gentiles he never forgot the fact that he was a member of the tribe of Benjamin and a Hebrew, he still retained a special relationship with the Jews. The Lord Jesus Christ was the realisation and fulfilment of the true Jewish religion. In the entire plan that God had for humanity, He worked, firstly, through the Jew and then in His most significant act He sent His own Son. The Son, therefore, becomes the pinnacle of God's entire plan.

Before God began to create, He knew that man, created in His own image, would sin and that He had already developed a plan of salvation. “For he chose us in him before the creation of the world to be holy and blameless in his sight.” (Ephesians 1: 4 NIV)

God’s major purpose was not that those who rejected Him should spend eternity in the Lake of Fire. For, when He first made Adam He consulted with Him over the names of all the creatures and then He walked with Adam and Eve, enjoying fellowship with them in the garden.

One good way of seeing what God had in mind is to look to the end of time and see how He works out His almighty purpose. In Revelation 19 we have the marriage supper of the Lamb. In one of the crowning moments of time the Lamb comes to take His bride. Now, the bride is the church and Christ is the Lamb. The Lord commanded husbands to love their wives in the same way that Christ loved the church. If the church is to become the bride of Christ then the church was made to be loved by Christ, Who is Almighty God.

We are created to be loved by God and to enjoy that love but in order to increase our enjoyment of that love God gave us the ability to choose to enjoy that love. When someone is given a choice there is the expectation that either option may be chosen. For those who choose to enjoy that love, God is faithful and will always give them what they have chosen. Even though God is absolutely powerful and can do anything; He has restricted Himself in that He is always consistent and keeps His promises. God will not lose faith with those who choose to enjoy His love so that those who choose not to enjoy His love can be insulated from the fruit of their choice.

There is, however, a problem "for all have sinned and fall short of the glory of God." (Romans 3: 23 NIV) How can we enjoy the God's love if we are sinners and our sins have separated us from our God? Well, this is where the Lord Jesus Christ comes in. He is the perfect sinless man who is not separated from God. As a sinless man, He is able to have fellowship with God and is also able to become a substitute for sinners. Without the Lord Jesus Christ, the Lord's plan of allowing people to enjoy His love fails for sin separates.

Our Saviour, the Lord Jesus Christ is the fulcrum of time. God's entire plan stands on Him and His sinless life that was followed by His atoning death and triumphant resurrection. Without Him, creation and time lose all their meaning and become a random series of destructive events. Praise God, the Lord Jesus Christ did involve Himself in time and give meaning to everything. He is, surely, the first and most important Man in God's entire plan for creation and humanity.

First In Rank

As we read about the Lord Jesus Christ, His earthly life and the subsequent events we soon realise that He was perfectly human but at the same time He is Divine. John, the apostle, begins by telling us that "the Word was God . . . Through him all things were made; without him nothing was made that has been made." (John 1: 1, 3 NIV) Paul, the apostle adds to this by saying, "Who, being in very nature God, did not consider equality with God something to be grasped." (Philippians 2: 6 NIV) There can be no other meaning to this than the fact that the pre-existent Word was Divine in every sense. No other man in all of history is Divine. Christ Jesus, Himself, made this claim. For example, He said, "Before Abraham was I AM." (John 8: 58)

There is no Biblical record of any other man claiming to be Almighty God nor is there a record of any other man being God. The Lord Jesus Christ was a unique man in that He is the only man in history who is God. Many other religions have records of their gods who behave with human frailty and some have records of men who achieve divine status because of the deeds they have done. Nowhere else do we have a record of Almighty God the Creator, becoming a man so that He could save His people from their sins.

Anyone who reads the Bible with an open mind has to accept the fact that the Bible affirms that the Lord Jesus is God but was He truly a man? Again we only need to look at the words of the apostle John: "The Word became flesh and made his dwelling among us. We have seen his glory, the glory of the One and only, who came from the Father, full of grace and truth." (John 1: 14 NIV) Furthermore we can read these things about our Saviour: "Beyond all question, the mystery of godliness is great: He appeared in a body, was vindicated by the Spirit, was seen by angels, was preached among the nations, was believed on in the world, and was taken up in glory." (1 Timothy 3: 16 NIV) "Since the children have flesh and blood, he too shared in their humanity so that by his death he might destroy him who holds the power of death - that is, the devil." (Hebrews 2: 14 NIV)

This means that there was one person who was both God and man at the same time. As far as the Scriptures give evidence, and as the Word of God, their evidence is comprehensive and true, there was no other man like this One. So we can see that the Lord Jesus stands out from all the rest of humanity because He is the only person who is God.

Now, not only is the Lord Jesus God, but He is a special man as well. He is a priest after the order of Melchizedek. This is not an honour that a man chooses for himself but one that is conferred by God. According to the regular passage of time, each Aaronic high priest died and the job was passed on to another. There were some good high priests and there were others who were bad. The priest of this higher order continues forever. During the regular course of the religious calendar of the Jewish people, tithes and offerings were given to the priests because the Lord took their tribe as his own. But, these priests, while they were still unborn in Abraham, paid tithes to the Priest of the higher order and hence, paid tithes to the Lord Jesus Christ.

Not only is Christ Jesus a priest of this higher order, He is also the Son. When the King gives a feast, the highest place is reserved for His Son, His only Son. So we can see that of all the people who were ever born on this earth that the Lord Jesus Christ is the highest in rank. Even though He took upon Himself the form of a servant, He did not lose his position as the man of greatest rank.

The Lord Jesus said that John was the greatest person who was born of a woman but that the least person in the kingdom of heaven was greater than John the Baptist. Now this does not mean that The Christ was less that John the Baptist because He is the greatest in the kingdom of heaven. In fact, John himself said, “A man who comes after me has surpassed me because he was before me.” (John 1: 30 NIV) The New American Standard Version uses the words, “After me comes a man who has higher rank than I.” This just confirms the fact that our Redeemer is the person of the greatest rank who ever lived.

First In Value

While we talk about the rank of the Lord Jesus, we are brought to the point where we consider Him as the “Firstborn”. In any family the person designated as the firstborn is the person of the highest rank. There are special rules of inheritance for the firstborn. He is to be given a double portion of the inheritance, even though he may be the son of an unfavoured wife.

In Numbers chapters 3 and 8 we read how the Lord took Levi instead of the firstborn of Israel, after the blood of the paschal lamb had saved them. So, in this sense, Levi became the firstborn of Israel and they were cared for by the gifts and offerings that were given to the Lord. Levi, as a tribe, belonged to the Lord for His service. Eventually the firstborn of Israel became the king, David. Even though Reuben was the firstborn according to time, He forfeited the right and so did the next two sons, Simeon and Levi.

There is another aspect to being the firstborn other than being first in rank. This is illustrated in the story about king David told in 2 Samuel 18. In this instance, the king ran away from his son Absalom and his troop went to fight for him. David made it known that he was willing to go and fight with his soldiers but they said to him, "You must not go out; if we are forced to flee, they won't care about us. Even if half of us die, they won't care; but you are worth ten thousand of us. It would be better now for you to give us support from the city." (2 Samuel 18: 3 NIV) David, the firstborn of Israel, was worth ten thousand of his men. So we can see that the firstborn is of greater value than any other person.

Our Redeemer is called the Firstborn. At the time of His birth we are told that He was Mary's firstborn son. In this case, it is not so much the fact that He is first in rank but first in time that is stressed. If the Lord Jesus Christ was born of a virgin, by the Holy Spirit, then He had to be her first child. Never the less, He was also the firstborn in terms of rank.

Paul, the apostle, calls the Lord "Firstborn". He is the Firstborn among many brothers and the Firstborn over all creation. This means that the Lord Jesus is the most valuable person in both the church and creation.

Even though we all live under grace, there are still some rules that apply in an absolute sense to the world. Under God's absolute Law, there is a punishment where value must be paid for value. If a person takes a life then his life is forfeit. The extension of this is simple. A person who sins against God must die. If God is willing to accept a substitute then the substitute must be of equal or greater value before the demands of Justice will be satisfied.

If David was worth ten thousand of his followers because he was the king of Israel, how much is the Firstborn of all creation worth? Well, not only is He firstborn as a man but He has the Divine nature as well and that Divine nature is infinite. So the Lord Jesus Christ has infinite value; that qualifies Him to be the substitute for every person who has ever been born. If every person were to take advantage of the Salvation offered by the death of the Lord Jesus Christ, there would still be more grace left than was used up. The value of our Saviour is greater than the sum of the value of every other person from Adam to Armageddon. This is where the "whoever believes in Him" clause finds satisfaction under the Holy demands of Almighty Justice.

First In Being Precious

Not only is our Saviour the “Firstborn”, He is also known as the “One and only”. John, the beloved disciple, calls the Lord “One and only” five times. The only other times this word occurs in the New Testament is when we are told that Isaac was the one and only son of Abraham, the widow on Nain had an only son who was dead, the daughter of Jairus is an only child and the demon possessed boy is the only son of his father.

The idea of one and only seems to mean something other than birth as a primary focus. It means “of sole descent”, that is, having no siblings and stresses the fact that they have never had more than one child. Not only this, the word can mean, “unique”, "unparalleled" or "incomparable" though this should not be confused with references to species, class or manners.

In the Septuagint the word is used to translate a word meaning only one child as in the case of Jephthah's daughter. He came back from winning his battle and promised to offer the first person that came to meet him as a burnt offering. Jehphthah was heart broken because she was more precious to him than any other person.

In other places in the Septuagint this same Hebrew word is translated by a Greek word meaning "beloved". For Abraham, Isaac was certainly beloved as well as being the one and only son of his true wife and the son of promise.

In the New Testament, only John uses this word in relation to the Lord Jesus as the Son of God, while Mark and Luke talk about "My beloved Son". So we can see that the Lord Jesus is more precious before God than any other person. In His capacity as both Man and God, He is able to be the mediator between God and man. Precious on both sides for there is no other way that the relationship between God and man can be restored.

When God deals with man, He deals in a way that is against man's natural inclination. As the Lord Jesus acted at the miracle of Cana in Galilee, so He acts in relation with man. The best wine was served last when, under normal circumstances, a cheaper wine would have been served. This is a natural human response. We often seek to give less than what we get, we are happy if we can get better value than what we give in exchange.

God works in exactly the opposite way. He gave the most precious thing so that we, who are less precious, might be redeemed. Both as God and Man our Saviour is far more precious than any of the people He came to save yet He was willing to die in our place.

First In Ability

As we think about the first of the signs in John's gospel our minds travel on to the other signs as well. John uses the word "sign" to stress the value or significance of the miracles that he recorded.

These signs are: the turning of the water into wine at Cana in Galilee as we considered earlier.

After the Lord met with the woman by the well in Sycar, He returned to Galilee and was, subsequently, met by a nobleman with a sick son. This man begged the Lord to come and heal his son. Eventually the Lord told the man that his son was healed and when the man returned home he discovered that his son had been healed at the exact time when the Lord said that the boy was healed.

Our Saviour headed down to Jerusalem for a feast of the Jews. While He was in Jerusalem, He went to a pool called Bethesda. Even though it was the Sabbath, the Lord healed a man who could not walk. This poor man had waited in hope for thirty-eight years before the Master commanded him to take up his bed and walk. While there is no doubt that the Lord did a good thing for the man, He was persecuted by His enemies because He had "broken" the Sabbath. Of course, the Man who gave the Sabbath in the first place knew what was meant in God's mind and He did not really sin.

The next sign was the feeding of the five thousand, back in Galilee. Here the Good Shepherd fed some of His hungry sheep so that they would not expire from lack of food.

Immediately after this the disciples went into a boat and were soon swamped in the water and afraid for their lives. Before the seas could overwhelm the boat and take their lives, the Master came to them walking on the water and they were saved from this peril.

On another Sabbath the Lord found a blind man and put mud on the man's eyes. This man was soon seeing even though he had been blind since the day of his birth. This was another opportunity for the Lord's enemies to persecute Him because He violated their traditions concerning the Sabbath.

The next sign was one for the Lord's dear friends Mary and Martha who lived in Bethany. This time the Lord healed one of His best friends. This was no ordinary healing, however, because Lazarus had been dead for four days.

John tells us that the Lord Jesus performed many miracles and did many other things as well. So much so that if "every one of them were written down, I suppose that even the whole world would not have room for the books that would be written." (John 21: 25 NIV) He chose these seven special signs so that we "may believe that Jesus is the Christ, the Son of God, and that by believing we may have life in his name. (John 20: 31 NIV)

While John doesn't count the miracle of the resurrection as one of those signs, this is the greatest of all the signs. While it is true that other people were brought back to life after they had died, no one else was able to bring themselves back to life except the Lord Jesus.

Nowhere else do we find a man with enough ability to demonstrate that He is the Son of God and certainly no one else is able to give life through his name? Certainly, our Saviour is the first among all men as far as His ability is concerned.

The gospel written by John has an ninth sign in the epilogue. This is the time when the disciples were able to catch a huge load of fish after the death and resurrection of the Saviour. We can see from this that His ability was not diminished by the fact that He died. It goes to confirm that He was still in control of the elements of nature, even at the moment when He hung from the cross. The sun did not shine, at His command, during those dark and painful hours when He dealt with the penalty of my sin.

First In Willingness

John includes other information about this Man of unrivalled ability. He records some of the sayings of the Master as well. Seven special sayings are given significant mention by the apostle.

Seven times the Lord makes statements about Himself prefacing these with the words. “I am.” On an eighth occasion He just uses the word “I AM” to show that He is Divine. This Man of great ability is also God. Our Lord’s dual nature is a fact from which we can gain comfort from many times, even in one day.

Christ Jesus tells us that He is the Bread of Life. Everyone needs to have the basics for life and no one can survive without eating. The Lord Jesus knows this and He is able to supply all that we need as long as we are willing to trust Him.

We all need to have some direction in our lives. There is a popular saying today, "If you aim at nothing you are sure to hit it." These people forget about how Ahab was killed. More important than having something to aim at is seeing where we are going. People who are dead in their sins are in darkness. There is good news because the Lord Jesus Christ said, "I am the light of the world." We can all see if we want to.

The Lord Jesus tells us that He is: the Door of the sheep, the Good Shepherd, the Resurrection and the Life, the Way, the Truth and the Life and the True Vine. Each of these "I ams" illustrate a very important point. We have been finding out that the Lord Jesus is the most highly qualified person to be our Saviour but that is not enough. Not only does He need to be well qualified to do the job, He needs to be willing to do the job as well. A highly qualified Saviour who is not willing to be the Saviour is as bad as having no Saviour at all. Praise the Lord that the best Man for the job was willing to do the job. He freely chose to become the Bread of Life, the Light of the World, the Door of the sheep, the Good Shepherd, the Resurrection and the Life, the Way, the Truth and the Life and the True Vine. As sure as He lived, none of us was in a position to force Him to do any of those things. He was the first in being willing to save the world from sin.

First In His Desire To Be About His Father's Business

Little is written about the childhood of our Saviour. There is a group of birth stories and then His flight to Egypt and subsequent return to Nazareth. Perhaps the wise men came when the Lord was just less than two years old, as Herod had all boys less than two years killed. Maybe the young family used the gold, myrrh and frankincense to pay for their flight to Egypt. As devout Jews, all the correct procedures were carried out in the Temple and some aged saints were rewarded for their faithfulness.

Apart from the early life stories we only have one incident from the childhood of the Boy Who would one day hang on a cross for the sins of the entire world. The Boy

Saviour stayed behind in the Temple and was found hearing the doctors and asking them questions. He told His parents that He was to be about His Father's business (some versions have the young Christ saying that he was to be in His Father's house). There is no record of the things they talked about but did His perceptive questioning lead these learned men down the same path as He later took Cleopas and his companion while they walked on the Emmaus road?

Before the Saviour was born His earthly father was told, "You are to give him the name Jesus, because he will save his people from their sins." (Matthew 1: 21 NIV) The business He was about was the salvation of His people. That is why He came and that is what He died. We can only surmise but maybe, before all the hatred by leaders began, they had the chance to re examine the Scriptures in the light of the God Child's questioning and see what was really written there concerning Himself. Whatever the conversation, we know for sure that it concerned His Father's business.

Uppermost in His mind as He went to be baptised by John was the fact that He had a job to do. He said to the Baptist, "Let it be so now; it is proper for us to do this to fulfil all righteousness." (Matthew 3: 15 NIV) This was an essential part of His Father's business so the Lord went ahead with the plan.

Later in His life, our Saviour headed towards Jerusalem even though He knew that Jerusalem was the place where He would be killed. The sinless Son of God was heading towards Jerusalem where He would experience all the torments of hell yet it was His Father's business so He went. As He was preparing to give up His Spirit, the Redeemer cried out ""My God, my God, why have you forsaken me?" (Matthew 27: 46 NIV) There is only one place where a soul is completely cut off from God and this is the place of torment, so our sinless Saviour experienced the torments of being cut off from God on our behalf.

Every person who is redeemed by the Blood of the Lamb has good works that God has prepared for them to do. However, the Lord Jesus Christ had the most important work to do and He was devoted to doing this work. While He agonized in the garden, He had the opportunity to slip away into the darkness and leave His disciples to face the soldiers but He went to the soldiers Himself and allowed them to lead Him away.

No one was as dedicated to His Father's business like our Redeemer. In fact, without Him no one else would be in a position to call the Judge of all the earth Father.

First In Giving His Father Pleasure

So far we have been considering the Lord Jesus Christ and we have seen that He is better than any other person who has ever lived, or who will ever live. He is the first in rank, the most valuable and the most precious of all. Our Saviour is a man of unparalleled ability and He was willing to exchange all His goodness for us. This man is the very fulcrum of all God's plans and nothing exists without Him and His work.

Never the less, He was still a man in every way. How did God look upon this Man? In prospect, God had great regard for our Saviour. Many times, the Scriptures tell about

His prophesied coming. He is foretold as the Suffering Servant as well as the Coming King. We are told that He will be able to win the victory in His own strength.

When the Lord Jesus was born, the Father sent a host of angels to proclaim His birth. Even though He was born as a man, His heavenly Father rejoiced in His birth and sent an angel to tell the shepherds that he was bringing good tidings of great joy for all people. The Saviour had been born and was now lying in a manger in Bethlehem. As the Lord grew up He was well loved by all who knew Him because the Lord had blessed Him with a delightful personality. It was not until the Master began to threaten the authority of the corrupt leaders of the Land that they began to conspire against Him.

Our Saviour began His public ministry when He went to be baptised by John in the Jordan River. Until that time he was a humble carpenter in Nazareth quietly waiting to embark on His life's work. He went to see John and the Baptist was not willing, immediately to baptise Him. How remarkable that the Lord's cousin did not realise that He was the Saviour of the world until that moment.

As our Redeemer came up out of the waters of baptism the Spirit descended like a dove and rested on Him. At the same time, there was a voice from heaven saying, "This is my Son, whom I love; with him I am well pleased." (Matthew 3: 17 NIV) So, when the Lord Jesus began His ministry, the Father in heaven was pleased with what He was doing.

The Lord set out on His life's work. Many people begin their lives well but so often there is some kind of failure along the way and they do not continue as they began. King Saul began well but fell into sin and the Spirit of the Lord departed from Him. King

Solomon asked the Lord for wisdom to rule the kingdom when he was a young man but later he married many foreign wives and his heart strayed so that he was not loyal to the Lord like his father David.

This was not true of the Lord Jesus Christ. Later in His ministry, He went up to be transfigured in front of three of His disciples, Peter, James and John. At the end of that experience, God again proclaimed that He delighted in the Lord Jesus. He spoke out of the cloud and said, “This is my Son, whom I love. Listen to him!” (Mark 9: 7 NIV)

In the last week before He went to die on the cross, the Lord asked His Father to glorify His Name and the Father spoke again from heaven, “I have glorified it, and will glorify it again.” (John 12: 28 NIV) So, even in the last week of His earthly ministry the Lord was still proclaiming His satisfaction with the Son. Not only that, He reaffirmed that He would continue to be pleased with His Son and would glorify His Name again.

When John was an old man he was given a vision of heaven. There in heaven, the Lamb is praised for the fact that He did a good job. The heavenly host said of Him, “Worthy is the Lamb, who was slain, to receive power and wealth and wisdom and strength and honour and glory and praise!” (Revelation 5: 12 NIV)

Almighty God, the heavenly Father was pleased with His Son and the work that He had done. No one gave pleasure to the Father like His own Beloved Son.

First In Authority

While there were many men who did not recognize that the Lord Jesus was Divine, the demons seemed to have no trouble recognizing the fact that He is God.

Not long after the Lord called James and John, the sons of Zebedee to follow Him, He went into a synagogue in Capernaum on the Sabbath. The people there were astonished as He taught them because He was able to teach the Scriptures with authority, unlike their usual teachers. A man with an unclean spirit came and called out to the Lord, "What do you want with us, Jesus of Nazareth? Have you come to destroy us? I know who you are - the Holy One of God!" (Mark 1: 24 NIV) He knew that this man was also God.

When He said this, the Lord immediately commanded the spirit to come out of the man and the spirit was forced to obey. There was no way that this spirit could resist the Lord's authority and immediately it left the man.

On another occasion the Saviour was in the country of the Gadarenes and He was again met by a man with an unclean spirit. This time the man was completely under the evil spirit's control and he spent all his time wandering among the tombs and cutting himself with stones. No one was able to restrain this man even though they had tried to bind him with chains. As soon as this possessed man saw the Master, he began to worship Him. There was not just one spirit but also a whole legion of spirits in the man.

These spirits did not want to leave this country and they begged the Lord to let them stay. They had to obey even though they did not want to leave that place. There was a herd of pigs nearby and the demons entered the herd of pigs. Suddenly the pigs stampeded down the hill and fell over a nearby cliff and were drowned in the sea. Now the demons wanted to stay in that area and be sent to the pigs, but when the pigs were drowned the demons were returned to the abyss even though they did not want to go there. Not even this large crowd of demons was unable to resist the command of the Master.

On another occasion, the Master was in a ship with His disciples and they were assailed by a great storm. Even the fishermen among the disciples were scared that they would be killed. Some of the Lord's disciples had spent a large part of their lives on this very sea fishing in similar boats. They knew the sea and its conditions so they were not just panicking at a little bit of wind. This was a fierce storm but the Lord was asleep in the boat.

When the disciples woke Him up, He commanded the storm and it immediately stopped and the sea was calm again. This was not the only time that the Lord commanded the storm to stop. He was even able to walk on the water in the middle of one of these storms.

There have been other people who have been able to command unclean spirits to come out of people. For example, both Peter and Paul, the apostles, commanded evil spirits to come out of people but they always invoked the Name of the Lord Jesus Christ before they were able to do this. The Saviour had the authority in His own right to command the evil spirits and to command the elements of nature while no one else did. Surely He is, of all men, the One with the greatest authority

First In Perfection

Jesus, who was known as the carpenter, the son of Mary, lived in Nazareth from his early years until he was about thirty years of age.

There is a large plain that breaks the highlands of central Palestine. This wide fertile plain is called the Plain of Jezreel. This plain is surrounded by mountains and has formed a natural battleground over the ages. The highest mountain is situated on the west and on the lower slopes of the mountain we could find the small town of Nazareth. A great caravan route led through Nazareth so it was not a completely isolated rustic town but people from many nations would pass through its streets. It was also one the great centres of Jewish Temple life.

The learned Jews of Jerusalem and the great and powerful families of the capital would despise these people as being uncultured. They spoke with a different accent and were despised as unlettered country people.

Nazareth was just like any other small country town, even today. Everyone in the town knew everybody else and what they were doing. In small country towns today it is very hard to keep things a secret and even harder to stop the gossip. It must have been like that in Nazareth during the time that the Lord Jesus lived and grew to manhood there. The local people all knew His mother and the rest of His family and the fact that He was a carpenter.

It is very hard for a man with unethical business standards to survive for long in a small town without people knowing that he is a crook. Every day of his life, as He lived in this small town, the Lord would have been under the scrutiny of the local people. Everything that He made or repaired would be carefully tested to see if it was good or not. Why, when He got up to speak in the local synagogue they were offended because they knew that He had not studied in all the right academies.

In spite of all this, when the time came for the Lord to be judged by the leaders of the Jews they looked in vain for witnesses against Him. His life had been exemplary and they had to look for false witnesses but even they were not credible. Not only did He grow up in that small town but He spent about three years in the glare of the public spotlight.

Many times His enemies sought to trap Him so that they could mount a case against Him but they could find no blemishes.

Now, a sacrifice has to be without blemish. So the Lord Jesus was able to qualify as a sacrifice because He was completely without sin. In fact, He was the only Person who lived a life and did not sin. According to His standards, thinking about something is the same as doing it so we know that in all His life He did not even think one sinful thought.

The very best in the business attacked our Redeemer and tried to make Him sin but He did not succumb to that temptation. Instead, He took the Word of God and used it as an effective weapon to defeat the devil. Truly our Saviour is the first when it comes to perfection.

First In Caring For His Friends

As soon as the Lord Jesus began His earthly ministry, He called some disciples to follow Him. He spent many hours teaching these men and training them to be His witnesses. They did not immediately realise that He was going to die on the cross and they probably expected that He would be with them for a very long time.

He rebuked them when they needed rebuking and was patient with them when they were impatient. The disciples knew that He was the Master and they were under discipline but He was not like an ordinary teacher. Our Redeemer was showing them the way that He expected them to act. His disciples had to learn that He was their Leader and Teacher and the best they could do was follow His example.

Never the less, He told them that they were His friends when He told them, "You are my friends if you do what I command. I no longer call you servants, because a servant does not know his master''s business. Instead, I have called you friends, for everything that I learned from my Father I have made known to you." (John 15: 14, 15 NIV)

We were all made to enjoy God's love and, as members of the church, to become the bride of Christ. In the marriage relationship there should be friendship and communication. Christ, Himself, instituted this friendship and told us about Himself and the Father. Without His life, we would know nothing about God and we would not even realise that we are headed for a lost eternity.

Best of all, however, the Lord told His disciples, and us, "Greater love has no one than this, that he lay down his life for his friends." (John 15: 13 NIV) This is the pinnacle of friendship and love. He, the perfect Son of God, the Creator of all things, took our sins and made them as though they were His own so that He could die as our substitute. No one could possibly love their friends more than this.

David, the psalmist said this, "LORD, who may dwell in your sanctuary? Who may live on your holy hill? … He who keeps his oath even when it hurts," (Psalm 15: 1, 4 NIV) Even though it says of our Saviour, "who for the joy set before him endured the cross, scorning its shame, and sat down at the right hand of the throne of God." (Hebrews

12: 2 NIV) He still did embark on a course of action that was detrimental to His immediate health. He loved us so much that He endured this pain.

Not only did He show His love for His friends by dying on the cross, He understood that we would find it hard to continue without help every day. In order to help us live in a fallen world He sent another Comforter after He went away. This was because He did not want to leave us alone or to feel forsaken. Surely there is no one else like our Saviour when it comes to loving His friends. What a privilege to be numbered among His friends. Not because we deserve to be His friends but just because He reached out and found us when we were lost because He is loving and compassionate.

First In Keeping His Word

While the Lord Jesus said many things during His earthly life, there are three broad promises that He made.

His first promise concerned three days. In the first instance, He talked about Jonah and how he spent three days in the whale's belly. From there the Lord went on to promise that He would be three days in the heart of the earth. Our Saviour also referred to the Temple, saying that is they destroyed the Temple He would build it again in three days. Most people thought that He was talking about Herod's Temple but He was talking about the Temple of His body. The Redeemer specifically told His disciples that He would be rejected and killed but after three days He would rise again.

Even though the Lord made this promise, when it happened, His friends did not understand what was happening. Some of them came to the empty tomb and then they believed others, like Thomas, did not believe until they had seen Him for themselves. There were at least five hundred people who saw the risen Lord.

Christ Jesus sternly warned the Jews that their Temple and the great city of Jerusalem would be destroyed. He told them that their beautiful Temple would be so thoroughly destroyed that not one stone would be left standing on top of another stone. This prophecy was literally fulfilled when Titus destroyed Jerusalem and the Temple in AD 70.

During the last meeting the Lord had with His disciples before he died on the cross, He was alone with them in the upper room where they had the Last Supper together. Much of that time was devoted to teaching and preparing the disciples for the time when the Lord would no longer be with them. One of the outstanding promises of that period was that of the coming Holy Spirit.

Our Saviour told His disciples, “It is for your good that I am going away. Unless I go away, the Counsellor will not come to you; but if I go, I will send him to you.” (John 16: 7 NIV) Not only that but, just before He went back to heaven, He also told them, “But you will receive power when the Holy Spirit comes on you; and you will be my witnesses in Jerusalem, and in all Judea and Samaria, and to the ends of the earth.” (Acts 1: 8 NIV)

On the day of Pentecost, this promise was literally fulfilled. Acts chapter 2 tells us how the Holy Spirit came upon the early church as they met together in the upper room. Not only were they powerful in their preaching and witnessing they were also comforted. From that day forward these men, who were formerly timid and fearful, were powerful and courageous in the service of the Master.

When we think about the Lord Jesus keeping His word perhaps these words should govern our thinking, "Jesus did many other things as well. If every one of them were written down, I suppose that even the whole world would not have room for the books that would be written." (John 21: 25 NIV) It would take more than an entire lifetime to discover all the promises that the Lord Jesus made and how they have been kept. Never the less, the three major promises that He made were fulfilled to the last detail. When anyone else makes a promise they are restricted in their ability to keep that promise for no one else is Almighty. If a person dies before they keep their promise then no one else may feel bound to keep it. God, on the other hand, will always keep His promises and no one is able to stop Him from keeping them.

First In The Power Of His Word

It was prophesied of the Lord Jesus Christ, "He was oppressed and afflicted, yet he did not open his mouth; he was led like a lamb to the slaughter, and as a sheep before her shearers is silent, so he did not open his mouth." (Isaiah 53: 7 NIV) This prophecy came true when He was led away from the garden of Gethsemane and He did not fight the troops who came to arrest Him.

When the Lord Jesus first approached these soldiers, He said unto them, "Who are you looking for?" They answered him, "Jesus of Nazareth." Jesus saith unto them, "I am He." As soon then as he had said unto them, "I am He", they went backward, and fell to the ground. Here they were falling to the ground at the force of His personality and His words yet, later, they led Him away and He did nothing to fight against them. These soldiers did not have the power to bind Him; He went with them because it was part of His own plan. (see John 18: 1-11)

As we think of these soldiers and the Jewish leaders arrogantly taking the Lord away, we can remember that He is God as well as being that humble man. Only One can destroy the body and soul in Hell, yet these people led Him away as though they had the power to do so. Surely He was the most gracious man Who ever lived.

That voice which was silent was the voice that commanded all things to come into being. Everything that was created was under that authority of His voice. The boiling cauldron of the sun sprung into being at His command and continues to burn at His command. He is the sustainer of all things and, were He to lose concentration for just one second; they would all cease to exist. Some of His creatures were busy rejecting His authority yet He maintained their world and their very lives.

His was the voice that calmed the sea and sent the unclean spirits rushing back to the abyss. None of them could resist the power of His word. Twelve legions of angels were ready to come and destroy all His enemies but they could not because the command to attack did not enter His mind.

Now the word of God is called a sword which is “able to penetrate even to dividing soul and spirit, joints and marrow; it judges the thoughts and attitudes of the heart.” (Hebrews 4: 12 NIV) At the end of this age, this sword will rule all the nations with an iron sceptre after this sword has slain the Lord's enemies at once. (see Revelation 19: 20, 21)

How amazing that for those critical hours when our salvation was in question this powerful voice remained silent and we were saved from our sins. His voice had the power to stop the sun from shining but His love kept Him on the cross so that He could pay the penalty for our sins. Some of our Saviour's enemies mocked Him, "You who are going to destroy the temple and build it in three days, save yourself! Come down from the cross, if you are the Son of God!" (Matthew 27: 40 NIV) Yet it was because He is the Son of God that He stayed on the cross to save sinners from their sin. His is the most powerful voice in existence but He held His peace so that we could be redeemed. What a Saviour!

First In A Job Well Done

We have demonstrated that the Lord Jesus Christ is the best possible candidate to be our Saviour. A Saviour needs to be perfect in every way so that He can become a substitute and He needs to be of at least equal value before He can act as a substitute. The Lord Jesus Christ lived a sinless life and He qualified as the perfect substitute. This man is more valuable and more precious than any other person who ever lived; in fact, He is of far greater value than the sum of the value of every other person who ever lived.

Our Saviour is not only the best qualified but He was willing to do the whole job. When the Saviour set out to purchase our salvation, He did not send someone else in His place but He came Himself. From the very beginning the plan called for the Best and it was the Best Who came. This Saviour did not need any help to do His job because He was able to win the victory by His Own strength.

Dr Tarrasch, a great chess expert once said, “It is not enough to be a good player, you have to play well.” It is not enough to have the best possible Person, Who is also willing to do the job. Sometimes the best person has a bad day and does not do the best possible job. So, what sort of job did the Lord Jesus do when it came to purchasing our salvation?

Before He came it was said of Him, “He shall see of the travail of his soul, and shall be satisfied: by his knowledge shall my righteous servant justify many; for he shall bear their iniquities.” (Isaiah 53: 11 KJV) The Suffering Servant was looking forward to the time when He would be wounded for the transgressions of the world. It is said of Him that He will be satisfied with the work that He has done. Now we know that this Suffering Servant is also Almighty God come as a Man. For God to be satisfied the job must be perfect. God, Who is perfect Himself, is not satisfied with anything that is less than perfect. In fact, if anything with a blemish is offered as a sacrifice it is an abomination to the Lord. While this was said of sacrificial animals it is also true of tasks completed. The Lord does not approve of anything that is less than perfect and He certainly is not satisfied with anything that is less than perfect. So for God to be satisfied with the travail of His soul then it must have accomplished all its purposes.

John the apostle tells us, “If we confess our sins, he is faithful and just and will forgive us our sins and purify us from all unrighteousness.” (1 John 1: 9 NIV) All we have to do is own our sins and then they are forgiven and we are made clean before God. How incredible, to have the option of confessing at any time. Peter asked the Lord how many times he would have to forgive his brother in any day and was told, “seventy times seven”. Now there are more than 6 billion people on the earth today and if each one of them was sin seventy times seven in a day and confess then the Lord would still have enough grace to forgive each one of those sins. This means that we have unlimited access to infinite grace and all this as a consequence of the death of the Lord Jesus Christ.

One death and resurrection and there is forgiveness for sin for all time. This forgiveness is more than just an entry condition to the kingdom of heaven; any person who sins, even as a Christian can confess and be forgiven. Each day we are given the choice of being clean before Him and having access to His love. This one act is good enough for eternity.

When the Lord Jesus Christ died on the cross to save us from our sins, He accomplished everything that He set out to do. Of all the tasks ever embarked on in history, this one was the one that was accomplished most completely. We have the best possible Saviour and He has done the best possible job when it came to securing our perfect salvation.

Firstborn From Among The Dead

Often, when a rich person dies they carefully plan their will before they die. Sometimes the person changes their will many times as one or another relative offends them in some way or another. After the person dies and the will is read some of the potential beneficiaries may be angry at the way the money was distributed. If this is the case, they will challenge the will and then the courts decide how the money is to be shared between the relatives.

When someone has died they are no longer in a position to ensure that their wishes are met. Even if they have the best lawyers in the world and all their money is put away in airtight trusts their wishes may not live on. One or two hundred years later the person will probably be forgotten and their wishes will certainly have no force.

Adolf Hitler, for example, was the supreme ruler of Nazi Germany and he used all his authority to destroy the Jews. He is now dead and the major outcome of his efforts was the formation of the state of Israel. Those terrible years when six million Jews were put to death put the Jewish people in a position where they decided that they had to have their own state to ensure that such a thing would never happen again. Of course, the Lord had prophesied that this state would be re-established thousands of years before.

When the Lord Jesus Christ died He did so leaving some of His promises yet to be fulfilled. He had some plans for His people even though He had virtually no earthly estate to distribute. After the soldiers took their share of His clothing there was nothing left for anyone else to share. This was probably a good thing because His clothes would soon have become like the bronze serpent that Moses made, objects for worship.

All these things soon became irrelevant because the Lord Jesus rose from the dead. He is called the Firstborn from the dead. Of all the people who died, the Lord Jesus has the greatest honour and the highest rank. Not only that, He is alive again and one day the church will rise to be with Him forever and He will still be the Firstborn among all that great company.

We are in the most blessed position possible. All those who come to the Lord Jesus Christ, by the power of the Holy Spirit, have the best possible Saviour, Who has done the best possible job and He has risen from the dead to ensure that all His promises are kept.

And not only that, He is Almighty God so that there is no one who is more powerful than He to make Him change His mind.

The quality of a person's salvation is directly related to the quality of their Saviour. Our Saviour is the best possible Saviour so we can confidently claim to have the best possible salvation. There is no greater honour on earth than that of being a sinner who is saved by grace.

Every day in every possible circumstance we can always return to the foot of the cross and enjoy the goodness of our Saviour's love. The prophet Isaiah wrote these words, "Thou wilt keep him in perfect peace, whose mind is stayed on thee: because he trusteth in thee." (Isaiah 26: 3 KJV) We can always have peace of mind if we spend time every day at the foot of the cross for that is the source of good will for daily living.

Did you enjoy reading this book? You could visit www.booksthataregood.com if you want to read more books by Doug McNaught.

www.ingramcontent.com/pod-product-compliance
Ingram Content Group UK Ltd.
Pitfield, Milton Keynes, MK11 3LW, UK
UKHW012233240726
13966UKWH00003B/1085

9 781847 995032